KIDS' COOKBOOK

KIDS' COOKBOOK

A first step-by-step book for young cooks

Ebury Press
London

First published in 2001

3 5 7 9 10 8 6 4

First published by Ebury Press
Random House, 20 Vauxhall Bridge Road, London SW1V 2SA

Random House Australia (Pty) Limited
20 Alfred Street, Milsons Point, Sydney, New South Wales 2061, Australia

Random House New Zealand Limited
18 Poland Road, Glenfield, Auckland 10, New Zealand

Random House South Africa (Pty) Limited
Endulini, 5A Jubilee Road, Parktown 2193, South Africa

The Random House Group Limited Reg. No. 954009

www.randomhouse.co.uk

A CIP catalogue record for this book is available from the British Library

ISBN 0 09 187854 3

Recipes written and tested by Emma-Lee Gow
Additional text by Janet Smith
Designed by Alison Shackleton
Photography by Craig Robertson
Food styling by Julie Beresford
Styling by Helen Trent

Printed and bound in Singapore by Tien Wah Press

Contents

Introduction

Cooking is great fun, whether you do it together with friends or with the help of an adult, and eating what you cook is even better. I certainly enjoyed creating all the recipes for this book along with my two enthusiastic young helpers – Oli, who cooks and eats almost anything, and Hannah, who just loves making a mess. The recipes in this book are not meant to be complete meals, nor are they necessarily the sort of things you should be eating every day; they are simply a collection of ideas for fun things to cook on rainy days, or when friends are coming to tea, or when you feel like doing something different. Whether you eat the things you cook for lunch or tea, save them for your lunchbox, or simply wolf them down as soon as they are ready, is up to you.

I hope these recipes will appeal to you, whatever your age and cooking experience. If you haven't cooked much before, you should enjoy learning about mashing, mixing and chopping; if you've already done some cooking, I hope this book will give you some new ideas.

Emma-Lee Gow

Food and Your Health

It's important to develop good eating habits right from an early age. All of us need a constant supply of vitamins and minerals, as well as carbohydrates and protein, to function properly. When you're young, it's even more important because your body is still growing and developing. The best way to ensure that you get all of these nutrients is by eating a varied diet, so aim to eat as many different foods as you can. Eat fresh fruit and vegetables every day and drink milk, or fruit juice mixed with fizzy water, rather than canned drinks. Don't snack on crisps and sweets between meals so that you're not hungry when your meals are ready. If you find that you do get hungry between meals, have a yogurt, a glass of milk or a piece of fruit. And remember that it's very important to brush your teeth really well after any snack, not just after your main meals.

Healthy food isn't boring and you probably eat lots of it already. Things like baked beans or poached eggs on wholemeal toast (no need to put butter on the toast); grilled fish fingers with peas and mashed potatoes; corn on the cob; grilled homemade hamburgers with salad; baked potatoes; cauliflower cheese; pasta with tuna or tomato sauce; and of course yogurt and fromage frais with fresh fruit like bananas, strawberries or nectarines, are all familiar healthy foods. It's important to remember that things like crisps, chips, chocolate and sweets contain hardly any nutrients and most don't contain any at all, although we eat them because they taste good. There's nothing wrong with that, providing you eat them in moderation and that you eat other things too.

Of course, if you've made a batch of biscuits or a cake, you are going to want to eat them, but instead of picking at them as soon as they are cooked, why not save them for tea or invite some friends round to share them with you.

Safety in the Kitchen

1 Always get an adult to help you, or at least make sure there is an adult nearby to help if you need it. You must ALWAYS have an adult with you when you are using knives, handling anything hot or using a food processor or blender.

2 Wash and dry your hands before you start, and after handling raw meat or fish.

3 Be very careful when using sharp knives and scissors. Always keep your fingers well out of the way and concentrate on what you are doing. Always use a chopping board. Don't play with knives or scissors, and keep them well out of the reach of little brothers and sisters.

4 Be very careful when using a food processor or blender. The blades are very sharp and you must keep your fingers well away from them.

5 Never use the same chopping board for preparing raw meat or fish and cooked things, or things like salad ingredients which are going to be eaten raw.

6 Remember that the heat from the oven, grill or hob can burn. Be very careful and always wear oven gloves when putting food into or taking food out of the oven or from under the grill.

7 Don't put hot pans or baking tins on to anything that will scorch, like a polished table, or anything that will crack, like a tiled work surface. It's a good idea to put a chopping board or heatproof mat on the work surface next to the oven so that you can put hot pans, tins or dishes straight on to it when you take them out of the oven. Don't leave hot things where someone else might touch them.

8 Steam can burn as badly as direct heat, so be very careful when draining things like cooked vegetables, rice and pasta. Never carry a pan of steaming liquid across the kitchen.

9 Hot sugar mixtures and hot oil can also burn, so be extra careful when using these ingredients.

10 Don't forget to turn off the oven, grill or hob when you have finished cooking. Always wash the dishes and tidy up after cooking, not forgetting to wipe clean the work surface.

Cookery Notes

1 Get all the equipment and ingredients ready before you start.

2 Use either grams or ounces for weighing the ingredients for a recipe, not a mixture of the two.

3 When measurements are given in tablespoons or mls, use proper measuring spoons. All spoonfuls should be levelled off with a knife.

4 Use size 2 eggs unless it says otherwise in a recipe.

5 Each recipe gives an idea of how much it makes, but for some things like biscuits for instance, this will depend on how thinly you roll out the dough and the size of the cutters you use. You could use cutters the size of small saucers, or even bigger, or perhaps you might prefer to use tiny cutters no bigger than large buttons. It really is up to you whether you want to make just a few large biscuits or lots of tiny ones. For things like the Pesto and Parmesan Twists (see pages 16–17) and the Iced Gem Sponges (see pages 50–51), it is impossible to say exactly how many people they will serve, as it depends on your age and how hungry you are! The number of servings given on the recipes are therefore only a rough guide.

6 Each recipe includes a list of the equipment you will need to make it. These lists don't include basic things, like scales, measuring spoons and forks which everybody has in their kitchen anway.

Quick Recipes

All of the recipes in this book are fairly quick to make – but some are super-quick. So if you're really short of time, or if you are cooking with a younger brother, sister or friend who can't concentrate for very long, try one of the following; Garlic and Herb Bread (see pages 10–11), Quick French Bread Pizzas (see pages 18–19), Carrot and Cheese Star Sandwiches (see pages 20–21), Onion and Red Pepper Omelette (see pages 24–25), Banana and Peanut Smoothies (see pages 42–43) and Mini Pavlovas with Marbled Raspberry Cream (see pages 62–63).

Garlic and Herb Bread

SERVES 4–6

YOU WILL NEED
80 g (3 oz) softened
    butter
2 garlic cloves
small handful of fresh
    parsley
small handful of fresh
    basil
few long lengths of fresh
    chives
salt and freshly ground
    black pepper
1 long bread loaf, such as
    ciabatta or a French
    stick
AND
small mixing bowl
wooden spoon
garlic crusher
chopping board
kitchen knife
small knife
kitchen foil
baking sheet
oven gloves

Before you start, turn the oven on and set it at 220°C (425°F) gas mark 7.

2 Using a kitchen knife, slice the bread in half lengthways. With a small knife, spread the garlic and herb butter on the cut sides of the bread. Put both halves of the bread back together, wrap tightly in kitchen foil and place on a baking sheet.

1 Beat the butter in a small mixing bowl using a wooden spoon. Using a garlic crusher, crush the garlic over the bowl of butter. On a chopping board, chop the parsley, basil and chives and add to the garlic butter. Season with a little salt and pepper. Beat all the ingredients well together. Set aside.

3 Place the sheet in the oven and bake for about 15–20 minutes. Wearing oven gloves, take the baking sheet out of the oven and remove the foil-wrapped bread. Leave to stand for 5 minutes before unwrapping the parcel. Cut into thick slices and serve immediately.

Quick Tuna Kedgeree

SERVES 4

YOU WILL NEED
small pinch of salt
225 g (8 oz) quick cook
    basmati rice
3 eggs
6 spring onions
15 ml (1 tbsp) olive oil
210 g (7 oz) can of tuna
    flakes
45 ml (3 tbsp) double
    cream
3 eggs
large handful of flat-leaf
    parsley
salt and freshly ground
    black pepper
2 lemons
fresh parsley sprigs, to
    garnish
AND
2 large saucepans
sieve
kettle
slotted spoon
chopping board
kitchen knife
20 cm (8 inch) non-stick
    frying pan
individual serving plates

1 Bring a large saucepan of water to the boil and add a little salt. Stir in the rice and return to the boil. Place the lid on the saucepan and simmer for 12–14 minutes. Drain the rice through a sieve and rinse carefully with boiling water from a kettle. Drain again.

2 While the rice is cooking, lower the eggs gently into another large saucepan of boiling salted water. Cook the eggs for about 7 minutes. Using a slotted spoon, remove the eggs from the water and leave to cool. Peel the eggs, cut into quarters. Set aside.

3 On a chopping board, using a kitchen knife, roughly chop the spring onions. Heat the oil in a non-stick frying pan and gently fry the chopped onions for 1–2 minutes or until softened.

4 Add the cooked rice, tuna flakes, cream and hard boiled egg quarters to the frying pan. Season lightly with salt and pepper and heat gently for 2 minutes or until warmed through. Chop the flat-leaf parsley and stir into the rice mixture. Cut the lemons into quarters.

5 Spoon the kedgeree onto individual serving plates. Garnish with the lemon wedges and fresh flat-leaf parsley sprigs and serve immediately.

SAFETY NOTE
You will need help from an adult when boiling the water needed to cook the rice and eggs

Potato Wedges with Crispy Bacon and Cheese

SERVES 4

YOU WILL NEED
4 baking potatoes
8 rashers of smoked
    streaky bacon
a little vegetable oil
8 ready sliced pieces of
    cheese, cut in half
salt and freshly ground
    black pepper
AND
4 metal skewers
20 cm (8 inch) non-stick
    frying pan
slotted spoon
kitchen paper
oven gloves
chopping board
kitchen knife
baking sheet
pastry brush
palette knife
4 individual serving plates

Before you start, turn the oven on and set it at 200°C (400°F) gas mark 6.

1 Push a metal skewer through each potato – this speeds up the cooking process by about 20 minutes. Put the potatoes on skewers into the oven and bake for about 1 hour or until tender. You will need to get an adult to help or do this for you.

2 Meanwhile, gently heat the oil in a frying pan. Add the bacon to the pan and cook for 2–3 minutes or until crispy. Take the bacon out of the pan using a slotted spoon. Place on kitchen paper. Set aside.

3 Using oven gloves, take the potatoes out of the oven when tender. Set aside.

4 Turn the oven up to 225°C (400°F) gas mark 7. Put the potatoes on a chopping board and, using a kitchen knife, carefully divide each potato into 4 wedges. Put the wedges on a baking sheet and, using a pastry brush, brush each wedge with a little oil. Return the potato wedges to the oven and bake for a further 15–20 minutes or until crispy and slightly golden.

5 Using oven gloves, take the sheet out of the oven. Turn off the oven. Arrange a piece of cheese over each potato wedge. Using oven gloves, put the potato wedges back on the sheet and return to the oven. Leave the potato wedges in the oven until the cheese melts. Using oven gloves, take the sheet out of the oven.

6 Using a palette knife, transfer 4 potato wedges to each serving plate and top each portion with 2 rashers of crispy bacon. Season with salt and pepper and serve immediately with some rocket or salad leaves and a few cherry tomatoes.

Pesto and Parmesan Twists

Before you start, turn the oven on and set it at 220°C (425°F) gas mark 7.

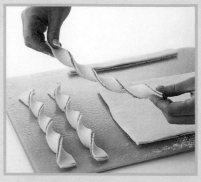

1 Sprinkle a work surface and rolling pin with a little flour. Roll out the pastry until it is very thin. Trim the piece of pastry into a neat shape, if necessary. Cut in half.

2 Spread one half of the pastry with an even layer of pesto, then sprinkle over the grated Parmesan cheese. Carefully lift the other piece of rolled-out pastry on top of the pesto and Parmesan cheese to make a sandwich.

3 Using a kitchen knife, cut the pesto and Parmesan pastry crossways into strips. Carefully pick up one strip and twist it around a few times. Put it on a baking sheet and press the ends down so they stick to the baking sheet – this will stop the twists unwinding as they cook. Do the same with all the other pastry strips.

4 Place the sheet in the oven and bake for about 10 minutes or until the twists are golden brown. Wearing oven gloves, take the baking sheet out of the oven. Leave the twists to cool on the baking sheet for about 5 minutes. Using a palette knife, carefully transfer the twists from the sheet to a wire rack to cool completely.

Quick French Bread Pizzas

Before you start, turn the grill onto high and the oven on and set it at 230°C (450°F) gas mark 8.

1 On a chopping board, using a kitchen knife, cut the baguette in half and then slice each half in two again lengthways. Place the baguette or pizza bases under the grill with the cut side facing down for 2–3 minutes or until lightly toasted. Thinly slice the tomatoes and crumble the cheese. Rub the toasted side of the bread or pizza bases with the cut side of the garlic. Arrange on a baking sheet.

2 Spread 15 ml (1 tbsp) of pesto over the surface of each piece of toasted bread or pizza base. Place a layer of tomato slices over the pesto then top with crumbled cheese. Sprinkle over the pinenuts, if using. Season well with freshly ground black pepper and drizzle over a little olive oil.

3 Place the sheet in the oven and bake for about 10 minutes or until heated through. Wearing oven gloves, take the baking sheet out of the oven. If you have used pizza bases, cut each pizza in half using a pizza slice or kitchen knife. Using a palette knife or fish slice, carefully transfer each pizza to a serving plate and garnish with basil sprigs.

Carrot and Cheese Star Sandwiches

1 On a chopping board, using a grater, grate the cheese. Put the cheese into a bowl and set aside. Using a vegetable peeler, peel the carrots, throw away the peelings and grate the pelled carrots into the bowl with the cheese. Using a small spoon, mix the cheese and carrots together well.

2 Spread a little of the mayonnaise on each slice of bread. Spread the carrot and cheese mixture over three slices of bread making sure you spread it right to the edges.

3 Using kitchen scissors, snip off a little cress, leaving the roots still in the punnet, and sprinkle it over the cheese and carrot filling. Press the remaining slices of bread on top to make sandwiches. Using a breadknife, cut each sandwich into 4 or using shaped biscuit cutters, cut the sandwiches into different shapes such as stars.

Onion and Red Pepper Omelette

Before you start, turn the grill on to high.

and onion. Heat half the oil in a non-stick frying pan. Add the chopped pepper and onion and cook over a low heat for 8–10 minutes or until they are soft.

2 Break the eggs into a small mixing bowl. Pick out any pieces of egg shell that have fallen into the bowl. Beat the egg lightly with a fork or hand whisk until the yolk and white are mixed together. Add the milk and a little salt and pepper and whisk together. Add the remaining oil to the pan and heat.

4 Transfer the frying pan to a preheated grill and cook for 4–5 minutes or until the omelette is firm enough to touch. Using oven gloves, take out the pan from under the grill and place the pan on a heatproof surface. Leave the omelette in the pan for a few minutes to settle.

5 Using a palette knife or fish slice, carefully slide the omelette from the frying pan onto a serving plate. Divide the omelette in half or cut into wedges. Serve immediately.

1 On a chopping board, using a kitchen knife, roughly chop the red pepper

3 Pour the whisked egg mixture into the heated pan and cook for 3–4 minutes or until the bottom is set.

Tuna and Chive Pâté

SERVES 4

YOU WILL NEED
- 210 g (7 oz) can tuna in oil or brine
- 8 long lengths of fresh chives
- 200 g (7 oz) full-fat soft cheese
- 1 lemon
- freshly ground black pepper
- granary bread or toast slices, to serve

AND
- can opener
- kitchen paper
- plate
- large mixing bowl
- grater
- lemon squeezer
- chopping board
- kitchen knife
- serving bowl
- cling film or kitchen foil

1 Open the can of tuna with a can opener or pull back ring. Drain away the oil or brine into the sink. Put some kitchen paper on a plate and tip the tuna out of the can onto the plate – the kitchen paper will absorb any the excess moisture. Flake the tuna with a fork and put into a large mixing bowl.

3 On a chopping board, using a kitchen knife, finely chop the chives and add to the tuna with the soft cheese. Mash all the ingredients together with a fork until well mixed. Spoon the mixture into a serving bowl. Cover with cling film or kitchen foil and put in the fridge until 30 minutes before it's required.

4 Remove the pâté from the fridge 30 minutes before serving. Serve with slices of granary bread or toast and a selection of watercress, fresh green salad leaves, fresh flat-leaf parsley leaves and cherry tomatoes.

2 Using a grater, finely grate the lemon rind and cut the lemon in half. Using a lemon squeezer, squeeze the juice from the lemon halves and add to the tuna. Season generously with pepper.

Lamb Burgers with Tomato Relish

MAKES 4

YOU WILL NEED
- 450 g (1 lb) plum tomatoes
- 1 small red onion
- 10 fresh basil leaves
- 1 garlic clove
- 45 ml (3 tbsp) olive oil
- 15 ml (1 tbsp) vinegar
- 450 g (1 lb) lean minced lamb
- 1 red onion
- salt and freshly ground black pepper
- 4 sesame seed buns
- 60 ml (4 tbsp) mayonnaise
- large handful of salad leaves

AND
- chopping board
- kitchen knife
- 2 large mixing bowls
- garlic crusher
- grater
- oven gloves
- fish slice

1 On a chopping board, using a kitchen knife, finely chop the tomatoes and red onion and put into a mixing bowl. Roughly tear up the basil leaves with your hands and, using a garlic crusher, crush the garlic. Add the basil and garlic to the tomato and onions. Add the oil and vinegar and stir well. Cover and set aside.

2 Put the lamb in another mixing bowl and mash with a fork to break up any large lumps. Using a grater, grate the onion and add to the lamb in the mixing bowl. Season with plenty of salt and pepper.

3 Divide the lamb into 4 and, using your hands, shape each piece into a burger. Try to make them all roughly the same size so they cook evenly. Preheat the grill to high. Arrange the lamb burgers on the wire rack of a grill pan and cook for about 5 minutes or until they are brown.

4 Using oven gloves, turn the burgers over with a fish slice. Make sure they are well cooked by cutting into the center of one and pressing down lightly – if cooked, the juices should run clear. If the juices are pink, cook the burgers for a few more minutes.

5 Spread 15 ml (1 tbsp) of the mayonnaise over the bottom half of each of the buns. Place a few salad leaves on top of the mayonnaise followed by a lamb burger and a spoonful of the tomato relish. Cover with the top half of the buns. Serve immediately.

French Bread Hot Dogs

MAKES 4

YOU WILL NEED
1 large onion
15 ml (1 tbsp) vegetable oil
8 chipolatas
1 large French stick
60 ml (4 tbsp) fruit chutney
4 ready sliced pieces of cheese
AND
chopping board
kitchen knife
20 cm (8 inch) non-stick frying pan
palette knife or fish slice
small knife
slotted spoon
bread knife

minutes or until the chipolatas are cooked through. Keep turning the chipolatas over whilst cooking to ensure they are brown all over. To check they are cooked right through, make a cut through a chipolata with a small knife and press lightly – if they are cooked then the juices will run clear. If the juices are pink, cook for a little longer.

1 On a chopping board, using a kitchen knife, cut the onion in half and then carefully cut each half into thin slices. Heat the oil in a non-stick frying pan, add the onion slices and cook for 2–3 minutes or until a little softened, stirring continuously. Using a palette knife or fish slice, push the onions into one half of the pan then add the chipolatas. Continue to cook the onions and chipolatas for 7–8

2 Turn off the heat and, using a slotted spoon, remove the chipolatas from the frying pan and put on a plate. Put the chipolatas aside. Turn the heat back on

and continue cooking the onions until very soft and brown in colour. Turn off the heat again and put the onions aside.

3 On a chopping board, using a bread knife, cut the French stick into 4 equal pieces. Carefully cut each piece in half lengthways, making sure not to cut all the way through the bread. Open out the bread piece by pressing on them lightly. Divide the cooked onions evenly between the opened out French bread pieces. Top each onion-filled bread piece with 2 chipolatas, spread over a little of the fruit chutney and a slice of cheese. Fold the French bread back to secure the filling. Serve immediately.

Chicken Caesar Salad

1 For the croutons, on a chopping board, using a kitchen knife, roughly cut the bread into small pieces. Heat the olive oil in a frying pan. Add the bread pieces and cook over a high heat for 3 minutes or until crisp and golden, stirring occasionally. Set aside to cool.

2 Using a potato peeler, hold the Parmesan in one hand and push the peeler away from you to make Parmesan shavings. Put on a small plate and set aside. On a chopping board, finely slice the chicken into bite-size pieces. Tear the lettuce with your hands into rough pieces, put into a large mixing bowl and add a little of the Ceasar salad dressing. Toss the lettuce until it is evenly coated with the dressing.

3 Pile the lettuce onto 4 large individual serving plates and top with some of the chicken. Scatter the croutons evenly over each plate and drizzle with the remaining dressing. Finally, sprinkle ech plate with the Parmesan shavings and season with pepper.

Fruit Rock Buns

Before you start, turn the oven on and set it at 200°C (400°F) gas mark 6.

egg lightly with a fork until the yolk and white are mixed together. Add the egg to the flour and fat and mix well. This mixture should be fairly firm but add a little milk if too dry.

a large mixing bowl. Cut the butter into small pieces and drop them into the flour. Using the tips of your fingers and thumbs, pick up a little of the flour and a couple of pieces of butter and rub them together to make the pieces even smaller. As you do this, let the mixture fall back into the bowl. Keep going until all the big lumps of fat have gone and the mixture looks a bit like breadcrumbs. (This technique is called 'rubbing in'.)

1 Pour a tiny drop of oil onto a baking sheet. Use a pastry brush to spread it all over the surface. Set aside.

2 Sieve the flour, salt, spice and nutmeg together into

3 Add the sugar, currants and peel to the flour, mixing them well together. Break the egg into a small mixing bowl. Pick out any pieces of egg shell that have fallen into the bowl. Beat the

4 Spoon the mixture into 12 small heaps on the prepared baking sheet, making sure they are evenly spaced. Place the sheet in the oven and bake for 15–20 minutes or until the buns are a light golden colour. Wearing oven gloves, take the baking sheet out of the oven. Leave the buns to cool on the baking sheet for 5 minutes. Using a palette knife, transfer the buns to a wire rack to cool completely.

Gingerbread Biscuits

MAKES ABOUT 12

YOU WILL NEED:
Vegetable oil for brushing
350 g (12 oz) plain white
   flour
5 ml (1 level tsp)
   bicarbonate of soda
10 ml (2 level tsp) ground
   ginger
125 g (4 oz) butter or hard
   margarine
175 g (6 oz) light soft
   brown sugar
1 egg
golden syrup
extra flour for sprinkling
currants or sweets
glace icing (see page 50)
or ready-made piping
   icing
AND
3 baking sheets
pastry brush
mixing bowl
knife, fork and spoon
small bowl
rolling pin
biscuit cutters (people,
   bears)
wire cooling rack

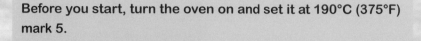

Before you start, turn the oven on and set it at 190°C (375°F) mark 5.

1 Pour a tiny drop of oil on to a baking sheet, then use a pastry brush to brush it all over the surface. Do the same to two more baking sheets.

2 Put the flour, bicarbonate of soda and ginger in a mixing bowl and mix together. Cut the butter or margarine into very small cubes and add them to the flour. Using the tips of your fingers and your thumbs,

pick up a little of the flour and a couple of pieces of butter or margarine, and rub them together to make the pieces of butter or margarine even smaller. As you do this, let the mixture fall back into the bowl. Keep rubbing the ingredients together until all the big lumps have gone. (This technique is called 'rubbing in'.) Mix in the sugar.

3 Crack the egg open on the side of a small bowl and let all the egg run into the bowl. If any pieces of egg shell fall into the bowl, pick them out with a spoon or with a larger piece of the broken shell. Hold a metal tablespoon in hot water for a couple of minutes, shake it dry, then quickly use it to spoon 60 ml (4 tbsp) syrup out of the tin and into the bowl with the egg. Because the spoon is warm, the syrup won't stick to it.

4 Using a fork, mix the syrup and egg, then pour into the flour mixture. Mix everything together and tip it out on to the work surface sprinkled with a little flour. Squeeze everything together with your hands to make a dough.

5 Cut the dough in half. Sprinkle a rolling pin with flour and roll out one half of the dough until it is very thin. Using biscuit cutters, cut out gingerbread men and women and teddy bears. Use currants or sweets to make eyes and buttons. Carefully lift the biscuits on to the oiled baking sheets. Roll out the other half of the dough and cut out more biscuits. Bake all the biscuits in the oven for 12-15 minutes or until the biscuits look a little darker in colour (don't worry if they seem soft – they will become crisp as they cool). Transfer the biscuits to a wire rack to cool completely. When the biscuits are cold, decorate them with icing and sweets.

Little Shortbread Biscuits

Before you start, turn the oven on and set it at 170°C (325°F) gas mark 3.

thumbs, pick up a little of the flour and a couple of pieces of butter and rub them together to make the pieces even smaller. As you do this, let the mixture fall back into the bowl. Keep going until all the big lumps of fat have gone and the mixture looks a bit like breadcrumbs. (This technique is called 'rubbing in'.)

2 Mix the sugar into the flour mixture. Sprinkle a work surface with a little flour. Place the mixture on top and squeeze it together with your hands to make a dough. Fold the dough over, press it down with your knuckles and turn it. Keep doing this until the dough forms a ball and becomes smooth and pliable. Pour a tiny drop of oil onto a baking sheet, then use a pastry brush to spread it all

1 Sieve the flour and salt together into a large mixing bowl. Cut the butter into small pieces and drop them into the flour. Using the tips of your fingers and

over the surface. Sprinkle the baking sheet with a little flour and set aside.

3 On a lightly floured work surface, using a rolling pin sprinkled with a little flour, roll the dough out to about 1 cm (½ inch) thickness. Using a selection of cutters or kitchen knife, cut out various shapes and carefully lift the biscuit shapes on the oiled baking sheet. Using a fork, prick all over the biscuit shapes.

4 Place the sheet in the oven and bake for about 40 minutes or until the biscuits are golden. Wearing oven gloves, take the sheet out of the oven. Leave to cool on the sheet for 5 minutes. Using a palette knife, transfer to a wire rack. When completely cool, sprinkle with caster sugar.

Banana and Peanut Smoothies

SERVES 4

YOU WILL NEED
5 ripe bananas
600 ml (1 pint) full-fat milk
75 ml (5 tbsp) smooth
   peanut butter
AND
chopping board
kitchen knife
plastic freezerproof
   container with lid
blender or food
processor
4 large individual serving
   glasses

SAFETY NOTE
Always ask an adult
for help when using a
food processor. The
blades are very sharp
and you need to take
extra care when
putting food in and
taking it out.

WARNING !
Never use any nuts,
including peanuts, if
anyone with a nut
allergy is going to
have a taste.

Before you start, ask someone to switch the freezer to 'fast freeze'.

1 Peel 4 bananas. Slice the bananas on a chopping board, using a kitchen knife, and put into a plastic freezer-proof container. Replace the lid and freeze for at least 2 hours but preferably overnight.

3 Peel the remaining banana. On a chopping board, using a kitchen knife, roughly chop the banana into chunks. Pour the smoothie purée into 4 large individual serving glasses and top with a little of the chopped banana. Finally, don't forget to tell someone to turn the freezer back to 'normal'.

2 Put the frozen banana, milk and peanut butter together in a food processer and purée until smooth.

Coconut Pyramids

MAKES ABOUT 16

YOU WILL NEED
2 eggs
125 g (4 oz) caster sugar
180 g (6 oz) desiccated
  coconut
2–4 sheets of rice paper
icing sugar for dusting
AND
large mixing bowl
small mixing bowl
hand or electric whisk
large tablespoon
2 baking sheets
oven gloves
wire rack
sieve

Before you start, turn the oven on and set it at 150°C (300°F) gas mark 2.

small mixing bowl. Repeat again with the second egg. Pick out any pieces of shell that have fallen into the bowl.

each sheet to cover its surface. Make the coconut pyramids by placing 8 spoonfuls of the mixture onto one of the baking sheets, making sure the pyramids are evenly spaced. Repeat with the remaining coconut mixture to make another 8 pyramids on the other baking sheet.

2 Using a hand or electric whisk, beat the egg whites until they are thick and form soft peaks. This will take quite and while and will make your arm ache if you're using a hand whisk – but keep going. When the mixture is ready, you should be able to turn the bowl upside-down without the egg white falling out. Now spoon in the sugar and whisk the egg whites again very thoroughly. Using a large tablespoon, mix in the dessicated coconut.

4 Place the sheets in the oven and bake for about 1 hour or until the pyramids are pale brown. Wearing oven gloves, take the sheets out of the oven. Leave the coconut pyramids to cool on the sheets then pull away the rice paper and place on a wire rack to cool completely. Dust each pyramid with a little icing sugar through a sieve before serving.

1 Crack one of the eggs on the side of a large mixing bowl and let just the white drop into the bowl through the half-open egg shell. Keep the yolk in the half shell until all the white has drained into the bowl, then put the yolk into a

3 Use the rice paper to line two baking sheets by placing the paper on top of

Orange Flapjacks

MAKES 18

YOU WILL NEED
vegetable oil for brushing
1 large orange
250 g (9 oz) unsalted
   butter, cut into small
   pieces
250 g (9 oz) golden
   caster sugar
175 g (6 oz) golden syrup
425 g (15 oz) porridge
   oats
AND
19 x 27 cm (10½ x 7½
   inch) baking tin
pastry brush
citrus zester
large heavy-based
   saucepan
wooden spoon
palette knife
oven gloves
chopping board
kitchen knife

NOTE
The best way to weigh
out the syrup is to first
measure out the sugar
and leave it in the scales
bowl, make a small well in
the centre of the sugar,
readjust the weights and
then measure out the
syrup. This means the
sugar and syrup will slide
easily into the saucepan.

Before you start, turn the oven on and set it at 180°C (350°F) gas mark 4.

1 Pour a few drops of oil into a baking tin, then use a pastry brush to spread it all over the inside. Set aside.

2 Place a citrus zester against the orange and draw firmly towards you to remove the orange rind in fine strips. Put into a large heavy-based saucepan with the butter pieces, sugar and syrup. Turn the heat on very low and cook the mixture gently, stirring all the time with a wooden spoon, until the butter has melted and sugar and syrup have dissolved.

3 Remove the saucepan from the heat and stir in the oats. Mix thoroughly until the oats are evenly coated in the syrup. Spoon the mixture

into the baking tin. Level the surface with a palette knife.

4 Place the tin in the oven and bake for 25 minutes or until the flapjacks are golden around the edges, but slightly soft in the centre. Wearing oven gloves, take the tin out of the oven. Leave the flapjacks to cool in the tin for about 10 minutes or until almost cold, then turn out onto a chopping board and cut into 18 bars.

Eton Mess

1 Choose a few nice looking small whole strawberries and set aside. Remove the green tops from the rest of the strawberries and throw the tops away. Using a kitchen knife, chop the strawberries on a chopping board and place in a large mixing bowl with the cranberry juice. Cover the bowl with cling film or kitchen foil and put into the fridge until ready to use.

a hand or electric whisk, stir the cream round and round very quickly until it gets a bit thicker and stands in soft peaks. Put the meringues into a plastic food bag and roughly crush the meringues using a rolling pin.

3 Using a large spoon, gently fold the strawberries, their juices and the crushed meringues into the whipped cream.

4 Spoon the strawberry and cream mixture into a large glass serving dish or individual glass serving dishes and decorate with the strawberries you set aside earlier. Serve immediately.

2 When it's time to eat, put the cream in a large mixing bowl and, using either

Iced Gem Sponges

MAKES ABOUT 8–10

1 large ready-made
   sponge flan case
1 tube of ready-made
   icing with nozzles
1 packet of Baby Iced
   Gems biscuits
AND
selection of biscuit
   cutters

shape depending on its size. Work quickly as the icing sets fast. Attach 1–3 Baby Iced Gems biscuits to the icing and press down lightly.

is too thick, add a little more water, but not too much or the icing will run off the sponge cakes or biscuits. To check whether the icing is too thin, dip the wooden spoon into the icing, lift it out with the back of the wooden spoon facing upwards and see if the icing stays on the spoon in a thin coating. If the icing runs off the spoon it's too thin and runny. To thicken the icing, sift in a little extra icing sugar.

TO MAKE YOUR OWN
GLACÉ ICING FOR
CAKES AND BISCUITS

YOU WILL NEED
225 g (8 oz) icing sugar
about 30 ml (2 tbsp)
   warm water
AND
sieve
large mixing bowl
wooden spoon

1 On a work surface, using a selection of cutters, cut out shapes from the sponge flan case. Carefully move each shape after cutting. Make sure you cut the shapes close together so you don't waste too much sponge. The amount you make will depend on the size of the cutters.

2 Take the tube of ready-made icing and attach the star nozzle. Squeeze 1–3 blobs of icing onto a sponge

1 Sieve the icing sugar into a large mixing bowl – this makes the icing less lumpy.

2 Pour a little of the warm water into the icing sugar and mix with a wooden spoon to make a smooth glossy paste. If you think the mixture

3 Glacé Icing can be used to top fairy cakes, both baked at home or ready-made, sponge cakes or biscuits. Decorations such as

your favourite sweets,
chocolate drops, chocolate
strands and any other
chocolate decorations can
be stuck into the icing once
spread on the cake, but
make sure you do this
straight away as the icing
sets very quickly.

51

OTHER IDEAS FOR COLOURINGS AND FLAVOURINGS

To colour the Glacé Icing add a few drops of food colouring to the icing mixture after the water has been added.

If you fancy chocolate icing then sift 15 ml (1 tbsp) cocoa powder into the bowl with the icing sugar before you add the water.

For fruit flavour icing add 30 ml (2 tbsp) fruit juice, such as orange, lemon or lime, to the icing sugar instead of water.

Chocolate Walnut Brownies

Before you start, turn the oven on and set it at 180°C (350°F) gas mark 4.

1 Pour a few drops of oil into a square cake tin. Use a pastry brush to spread it all over the inside. Sprinkle the tin with a little flour. Set aside. Put the chocolate and butter in a small heatproof bowl. Put a little water in saucepan and heat gently until it simmers. Stand the bowl over the water making sure it does not touch the hot water. Turn the heat down to very low. Using a wooden spoon, stir the chocolate and butter until it has melted. Remove the pan and stir in the sugar. Set aside.

2 Sieve the flour and salt together into a large mixing bowl. Break the egg into a small mixing bowl. Pick out any pieces of egg shell that have fallen into the bowl. Beat the egg lightly with a fork until the yolk and the white are mixed together. Add the vanilla extract. Set aside.

3 On a chopping board, roughly chop the walnuts using a kitchen knife. Set aside.

4 Add the chocolate mixture, beaten eggs and walnuts to the flour. Mix well until smooth, using a wooden spoon. Spoon the mixture into the prepared baking tin and level the surface with a palette knife.

5 Place the tin in the oven and bake for 35–40 minutes or until the brownies are well risen. Wearing oven gloves, take the tin out of the oven. Leave the brownies to cool in the tin for about 10 minutes or until almost cold. Using a kitchen knife, carefully cut the brownies into 12 bars. Carefully remove the brownies from the baking tin using a palette knife.

WARNING !
Never use any nuts, including walnuts, if anyone with a nut allergy is going to have a taste.

Frozen Summer Berry Yogurt Ice

●●●●●●●●●●●●●●●●●●●●●●●●

SERVES 8–10

YOU WILL NEED

500 g (1 lb 2 oz) frozen
  summer fruits of the
  forest, thawed
120 ml (8 tbsp) icing
  sugar
30 ml (2 tbsp) runny
  honey
150 ml (5 fl oz) Greek
  yogurt
300 ml (½ pint) double
  cream
2 egg whites
AND
sieve
3 large mixing bowls
wooden spoon
cling film or kitchen foil
hand or electric whisk
large metal spoon
shallow plastic
  freezerproof container
  with lid

Before you start, ask someone to switch the freezer to 'fast freeze'.

through the sieve into the bowl. Add 60 ml (4 tbsp) of the icing sugar and the honey to the sieved fruits and stir until dissolved. Stir the yoghurt into the fruit mixture. Cover the bowl with cling film or kitchen foil and put into the fridge until ready to use.

large mixing bowl, and using a hand or electric whisk, stir the cream round and round very quickly until it gets a bit thicker and stands in soft peaks. Stir the whipped cream into the sieved fruit mixture. Now wash and dry the whisk.

1 Put the thawed summer fruits in a sieve over a large mixing bowl. Push the fruits through the sieve using the back of a wooden spoon. Throw away anything left in the sieve once all the juices of the fruit have passed

2 When it's time to eat, put the cream in a separate

3 Put the egg whites into another clean mixing bowl with the remaining sugar. Using the clean hand or electric whisk, beat the egg whites until they are thick and form soft peaks. This will take quite and while and will make your arm ache if you're using a hand whisk – but keep going. When the mixture is ready, you should be able to turn the bowl upside-down without the egg white falling out.

4 Using a large metal spoon, carefully fold the egg white into the sieved fruit mixture, making sure it is all mixed together evenly. Pour the mixture into a shallow plastic freezerproof container and freeze for at least 4 hours or until firm. When the yogurt ice is firm, put it in the fridge and leave for 10 minutes before eating. Finally, don't forget to tell someone to turn the freezer back to 'normal'.

Fresh Green Fruit Skewers

SERVES 4

YOU WILL NEED
125 g (4 oz) granulated
  sugar
1 lime
½ Galia melon
2 kiwi fruit
1 Granny Smith apple
175 g (6 oz) seedless
  green grapes
To decorate
fresh mint leaves
Greek yoghurt
AND
8 wooden skewers
shallow dish
citrus zester
chopping board
fruit juice squeezer
saucepan
shallow bowl
kitchen knife
apple corer
vegetable peeler
baking sheet
kitchen foil
oven gloves

against the lime skin and drawing it firmly towards you. On a chopping board, usinf a kitchen knife, cut the lime in half and, using a fruit juice squeezer, squeeze the juice from the lime.

3 Put the granulated sugar and lime zest in a saucepan with 300 ml (11 fl oz) cold water. Heat gently until the sugar has dissolved. Increase the heat and boil for 1 minute. Add the lime juice. Pour into a shallow bowl.

slice the flesh away from the peel. Cut into chunks. Cut the top and bottom off the kiwi fruits then peel using a potato peeler. Cut in half lengthways then across into thick slices. Core the apple, cut in half and then in half again, then cut into large chunks. Put all the fruits into the bowl with the lime syrup and leave for 5 minutes.

5 Preheat the grill to high. Thread the melon, kiwi, apple and grapes alternately onto the skewers. Put a sheet of kitchen foil on a baking sheet and arrange the skewers on the foil. Grill for 5 minutes, turning occasionally using oven gloves, until lightly golden. Using oven gloves, take the baking sheet from under the grill.

1 In a shallow dish, soak the wooden skewers in cold water for at least 30 minutes.

2 Using a citrus zester, remove the rind from the lime by placing the zester

4 On a chopping board, using a kitchen knife, cut the melon into 4 wedges and

6 Put 2 skewers onto each serving plate and drizzle over some syrup. Decorate with mint leaves and yoghurt.

Fruit Scones

MAKES 8

YOU WILL NEED
225 g (8 oz) plain flour
pinch of salt
2.5 ml (1 tsp) baking
   powder
55 g (2 oz) dried mixed
   fruit
40 g (1½ oz) butter or
   margarine
about 150 ml (¼ pint)
   semi-skimmed milk
flour for sprinkling
1 egg or a little milk, to
   glaze
to serve
150 ml (¼ pint) double or
   whipping cream
strawberry jam
AND
sieve
large mixing bowl
baking sheet
rolling pin
6 cm (2½ inch) plain or
   fluted cutter
oven gloves
2 small mixing bowls
hand or electric whisk
pastry brush
oven gloves
palette knife
wire rack

Before you start, turn the oven on and set it at 220°C (425°F) gas mark 7.

1 Sieve the flour, salt and baking powder together into a large mixing bowl. Add the dried fruit. Cut the butter into small pieces and drop them into the flour and dried fruit mixture. Using the tips of your fingers and thumbs, pick up a little of the flour and a couple of pieces of butter and rub them together to make the pieces even smaller. As you do this, let the mixture fall back into the bowl. Keep going until all the big lumps of fat have gone and the mixture looks a bit like breadcrumbs. (This technique is called 'rubbing in'.) Little by little, stir in enough milk to make a fairly soft, light dough.

2 Put a baking sheet into the oven and leave to

heat while you shape the scones into rounds. Sprinkle a little flour onto the work surface then, with a rolling pin, lightly roll the dough out to 2 cm (¾ inch) thickness and cut into rounds with a 6 cm (2½ inch) plain or fluted cutter.

3 Using oven gloves, remove the hot baking sheet from the oven and carefully lift the rounds on to the baking sheet. Break the

egg into a small mixing bowl. Pick out any pieces of egg shell that have fallen into the bowl. Beat the egg lightly with a fork until the yolk and the white are mixed together. Using a pastry brush, lightly brush the tops of the rounds with beaten egg or milk.

4 Place the sheet in the oven and bake for about 10 minutes or until the scones are golden brown and well risen. Wearing oven gloves, take the baking sheet out of the oven. Leave the scones to cool on the baking sheet for 5 minutes. Using a palette knife, transfer the scones to a wire rack to cool.

5 In a small mixing bowl, whip the cream with a hand or electric whisk until it beging to stiffen and soft peaks start to form. Serve the scones warm, split in half, with the two halves sandwiched together with a teaspoon of strawberry jam and a teaspoon of the whipped cream.

Mini Pavlovas with Marbled Raspberry Cream

MAKES 6

YOU WILL NEED
350 g (12 oz) fresh raspberries
15 ml (1 tbsp) caster sugar
300 ml (½ pint) double cream
200 ml (7 fl oz) Greek yogurt
6 individual ready-made mini meringues
a few fresh mint leaves, to decorate
AND
2 large mixing bowls
cling film or kitchen foil
hand or electric whisk
large spoon
6 individual serving plates

1 Choose a few nice looking small whole raspberries and set aside. Remove any stalks from the rest of the raspberries and place in a large mixing bowl. Add the sugar and crush the raspberries lightly with a fork. Cover the bowl with cling film or kitchen foil and put into the fridge until ready to use.

2 When it's time to eat, put the cream in a separate large mixing bowl, and using a hand or electric whisk, stir the cream round and round very quickly until it gets a bit thicker and stands in soft peaks. Add the yogurt to the whipped cream and then, using a large spoon, fold in the crushed raspberries.

3 Put the mini meringues onto 6 individual serving plates. Divide the raspberry cream mixture evenly and place in the middle of each meringue. Decorate with the raspberries you set aside earlier and mint leaves. Serve immediately.

Index